ANDREW MCNEILLIE was born in 1946 at Hen Golwyn and educated at the primary school there and at John Bright Grammar School in Llandudno. He read English at Magdalen College, Oxford, and is now Literature Publisher for Blackwell Publishing in Oxford. His collection of poems *Nevermore* (2000) in the Oxford*Poets* series from Carcanet was shortlisted for the Forward Prize for Best First Collection. *An Aran Keening*, an account of his year-long sojourn on Inis Mór, 1968–69, was published in 2001 by the Lilliput Press, Dublin, and in 2002 by the University of Wisconsin Press in the USA. He operates, with backing from Southern Arts, The Clutag Press, hand-setting and printing, in a series of leaflets, work by both beginning and established poets.

ANDREW McNEILLIE

Now, Then

Oxford*Poets*

CARCANET

First published in 2002 by
Carcanet Press Limited
4th Floor, Conavon Court
12–16 Blackfriars Street
Manchester M3 5BQ

A CIP catalogue record for this book
is available from the British Library

ISBN 1 903039 60 6

The publisher acknowledges financial assistance
from the Arts Council of England

Set in Monotype Ehrhardt by XL Publishing Services, Tiverton
Printed and bound in England by SRP Ltd, Exeter

In Memory of my Father

Acknowledgements

A number of these poems have appeared in: *Fortnight, Metre, Moving Worlds: A Journal of Transcultural Writings, Oxford Magazine, PNR, Poetry Wales, Thumbscrew, TLS, Yale Review*. I am grateful to the editors of these journals for allowing me the light of day in their pages. The group of poems 'Plato's Aviary (Puts Out a Wing)', together with the poem 'Rookery Nook' were published as *One for the Road*, a Thumbscrew Press pamphlet in 2002: I want particularly to thank Tim Kendall for generously bringing this about. Heartfelt thanks must go to: Angharad Price for her translation of 'Swallow' into Welsh and for allowing me to include it here; and to: Jonathan Williams and 'Poetry in Motion' for reproducing 'Swallow' as a Poets' Corner poster on the Dublin Dart commuter rail network; to Peter McDonald of Christ Church, Oxford, and the Christopher Tower Poetry web page, for including several of the poems here in the Poet of the Month feature, in January 2002. Peter Brown and David Wallace both know why they are especially thanked here.

Contents

Bye Bye Blackbird		11
Waiting for Woodies		12
The Three Guillemots		13
Back of Beyond		14
Dulyn		15
Dark Horse		16
Llyn-y-Foel		17
In Flagrante Delicto		19
In Youth's Dream-Time		20
Zencrake		21
Plato's Aviary (Puts Out a Wing)		
(i)	I Spy With My Little Eye	22
(ii)	Kittiwake	23
(iii)	Peregrine	24
(iv)	Goldfinch	25
(v)	Ring-Ouzel	26
(vi)	Grey Wagtail	27
(vii)	Moorhen	28
(viii)	Sandpiper	29
(ix)	Ringed Plover	30
(x)	Heron	31
(xi)	Swallow	32
(xii)	Jay	33
(xiii)	Chaffinch	34
(xiv)	Pheasant	35
(xv)	Kestrel	36
(xvi)	Magpie	37
(xvii)	House Martin	38
(xviii)	One for the Road	39
Bird Scarer		40
Once or Twice		41
Now, Then		42
Rookery Nook		43
Set Aside		44
Contra Heraclitus		45
Arboretum		
(i)	Silver Birch	46
(ii)	Heather	47

(iii)	Silver-Fir	48
(iv)	Furze	49
(v)	Rowan	50
(vi)	Ash	51
(vii)	Hawthorn	52
(viii)	Briar	53
(ix)	Hazel	54
(x)	Ivy	55
(xi)	Oak	56
(xii)	Holly	57
(xiii)	Dwarf Elder	58
(xiv)	White Poplar	59
(xv)	Alder	60
(xvi)	Willow	61
(xvii)	Elder	62
(xviii)	Yew	63

Headland 64
Belonging 65
Allt 66
Croeso 71
After Taliesin 72
In Vino Veritas 73
Hare 74
At Roundstone 75
American Wake 77
From Another World 78
Smogairle Rōin 79
Là-bas 80
Water Table 81
Meditation in Homage to the Playboy 82
Cimetière Marin 84
The Outbuilding 85
Lepus 86
Ploughs 87
The Blacksmith's Order Centenary 88
Father and Son 92
One More Time 93
The Way to Work 94
Weather Permitting 95
Harbourage 96
The Invective 98

8

Piss   99
Crying in the Wilderness   100
Prayer   101
An Oriental Tale   102
Half a Loaf   103
Elegy   104
A Watched Clock   105
At Walden Pond   106
The Shipwreck at Cape Cod   107
Near Mystic   108
Spring in Charlottesville   109
Birds of America   110
Blues in America   111
Appendix: Y Wennol: er cof am R.S. Thomas
          Translation by Angharad Price   114

Notes   115

'That the eye is necessary to sight seems to me the notion of one immersed in matter.'

J.S. Mill

'An eagle is said to know the place where it can find its prey, but not the time. A raven knows the time, but not the place.'

Giraldus Cambrensis

Bye Bye Blackbird

I heard them and listened spellbound.
Sometimes I would pause like one,
attending to some phrasing.
Or I'd sit waiting, hearing the silence
between lines, or stanza breaks.

So now with my pen poised:
the golden nib of my beak raised,
my thumbnail and index eyes staring
left and right, pricked to respond, I wait
on that other one across the stream.

Waiting for Woodies

(Columba palumbus)

I waited in those days until the evening thinned
All light away to distant strings and
Starry clusters, and a green pier-light
Blowing, like a bird's bright eye,
Away below, starboard on that seaboard.

It's not that I let anything distract me
At that wood's edge where I stood sentry.
Though I heard the odd one flutter home
Far behind me, and remembered the scent
Of cropped clover and barley.

And caught a kestrel briefly, anchored at
The corner of my eye, but kept my watch unblinking,
Through thick and thin, though rain spat sharply
And night loomed in. Still they wouldn't come.
As if something warned them I was there.

I've waited for poems in the same way since,
At the edge of things, in the heart's dark border.
And just as shrewdly they've stayed away.
Though I've caught sight too late
Of their shadows passing, on the way home.

The Three Guillemots

(*Uria aalge*)

The tank furred, and mottled like a frog,
With algae, and sooty to its depth, at first
Smelt musty, as the guillemots dashed and
Ducked and growled at us: 'arr...' 'arr...'
Releasing pungent dankness into the greenhouse.

They scissored my fingers raw as I tried
To feed them slivers of sprat and herring.
Who brought them to us I don't remember.
But we were that kind of people: a little wild,
Known to be knowing about the wilds.

Not as knowing as they thought, whoever they were,
Come up the lane that day, bearing three
Oil-clogged guillemots in a cardboard-box.
They'd stood there at the door, as if bringing gold
Or frankincense or myrrh, perhaps.

And waited, virtuously, like Jehovah's Witnesses,
Certain that, by the passage of his hand
Above the corner-over-corner tucked-tight lid,
The old man might, like the Lord Himself – or maybe
St Francis – save those guileless birds.

Back of Beyond

The signposts raise their arms
wonkily, as if to shrug they're lost too.

Their letters now scarcely legible,
mileages a faint memory.

Dulyn

i.m. John, Trevor and Ivor

To fish there you wade in air among
The rocks angling for your balance.

Black water chops ashore and the torrent
Holds you bubble-rapt in its sound-warp

Like a dipper submerged in a rushing pool
Intent on caddis larvae.

If one of the others came by to know
Your luck he could startle you to death.

Ghosts as they are, or not. They haunt here
Like the stories they told of ones that got away.

The steep cwm will catch your cast more
Than ever those wily fish might rise before you

To a hook ripped of its barb on a rock.
I learnt in this place, from the age of ten,

To curse like a man, 'God damn it to hell,'
To brew tea in a smoke of heather stalks and downfall,

To tie instant bloodknots and a noose
Round the neck of the Bloody Butcher

While the fish moved out of range
As now that world has veered forever

And every finger's a thumb, my reading glasses
Beaded with rain, and not a fish to be seen.

Dark Horse

Once, up there, before the stream, we found
A mountain pony's skull and jawbone
In the bog, and then the whole of it,
Just near the surface and dispersing
Like stars racing over the mountains.

On our way home we brought the skull with us:
To whinny in the dark of the outhouse,
And roll its eye, and show its teeth —
Its nostrils flared to scent the wilderness —
And dream like us of stars and mountains.

Llyn-y-Foel

True, I only went there twice,
But I was often there before,
And since. That we might go they'd air
In April or September, on the track down,
After a dour day.

It was best there early and late,
Fish tending to be lean, the water
Full of light, high
Above the workings in
The mist-shadow of Moel Siabod.

They'd weigh it up and I'd look
Across the way there, into the evening,
Longing for change. The grass is always
Greener where the heart's at home,
But where was that?

They'd done their adventuring way back,
When I was a twinkle in the old man's eye,
Like that first star. Now they were content
To pit themselves against the known,
And grow unknowing in perfection.

But I wanted my creel to spill
Tails and tales of my own, as of
Hard quarrymen, fishing it out
At Llugwy, on days in March so cold
Mere mortals would die there…

I wanted to cast my net on the other side
As now I want to make another kind of poem.
Those times we made the journey
It was like going on holiday,
And when we came home

There were wonders to retell. True,
Embellishment began there, and
What was true then is truer now
With just a mountainside to go,
The heart's creel creaking.

In Flagrante Delicto

(or 'Woodland Life, Wales', observed *aetat* eight)

Evening itself was young and the stream sultry,
seething with gnats and thunderflies.

I gazed across through the leaves to where
field drainage leached down among the trees:

I'd been there and I knew how thick the mud
could be at times, enough to suck your boots off.

That's where suddenly I saw them: her bare knees raised
and him between them clear to see through the saplings.

So once I had come upon Hughie Bach shitting,
his arse stuck out to the four corners of the earth.

In Youth's Dream-Time

'Social being gives rise to thought'
Terry Eagleton

He was waiting in the wings
In those days when the moon
Had currency like a shilling
New-minted in an owl's eye.

What stood between him and the world
He was at no loss to know.
He thought nothing of it because
He was it and couldn't not do.

Had you spoken with him he would soon
Look impatiently beyond you.
If he'd only seen you coming
He'd have already slipped away.

There was no other world for which
He could have entertained readiness.
He came home when he was hungry.
Well might he make you worry:

He lived as if there was no tomorrow
And tomorrow only. He could take
Whatever they threw at him.
Lessons flapped off the page or swam

Under his gaze, over his head,
Out at the window. Nothing woke him.
He knew none of it mattered,
His world was in other things.

He was waiting in the wings
In those days when the moon
Had currency like a shilling
New-minted in an owl's eye.

Zencrake

It's not easy to explain why
but whoever is inclined to say
because the mountain's there,
might know how it's the same
because the corncrake's not.

Plato's Aviary (Puts Out a Wing)

'The Admiral knew that the Portuguese had discovered most of the islands in their possession by observing the birds.'

Christopher Columbus, *Log Book*, Sunday 7 October 1492

(i)   I Spy with My Little Eye

How did they discover the rest?
Scanning for birds I guess.

(ii)   Kittiwake (*Rissa tridactyla*)

Here they come in a cloud matching
clouds of silver-white-grey, buoyantly,
crying *kitti… kittiwake…*

haunting the high crests and low
troughs of the heart in a paper-chase wake,
to make landfall where?

(iii)   Peregrine (*Falco peregrinus*)

All day fishing there I waited as much for its shrill *kek-kek-kek-kek*
kek-kek and scimitar soaring overhead as for the dimpling fish below.

How the day might drift on otherwise, the water hypnotic,
Light falling like manna, and all slap-happy in the rocks.

Every plane and facet of wave-mirror and cliff-hanging
Edge of expectancy, pitched there, in and out of the dream.

What sense trying to address the future? Whatever it contains
Won't include us. The art of waiting its métier as mine.

Once as we came back on an autumn evening, weary for the road,
School to face in the morning, homework not done, down one raced

In his scholar's gold rim glasses, and tear-smudged eye from too much study,
And thumped a grouse into the heather. Then, wings winnowing

And alarmed *kek-kek* for cry, it shot away, leaving us its prey,
The bird warm where we found it, severed from its head.

How much out of ten might I get for that? At fourteen, mind-wandering,
Learned only in the progress of the clock, in a world beyond time.

(iv) Goldfinch (*Carduelis carduelis*)

Still in these wild places, where
Scarce a human ever comes, they startle up
On sight, and wheel away, twittering and
Wheezing, smokily, buoyed up, like
Down, to land a meadow and a half away,
And flit among the starry thistleheads.

How you would prefer them to delay,
But in some earlier incarnation, I suspect,
They learned to distrust a species that
Will stoop to anything for gold: as those who
With pliers poised among the dead tweaked
Dental fillings out, as if by second nature.

(v)   Ring-Ouzel (*Turdus torquatus*)

Visiting cleric with a liquid sermon
(And rat-a-tac-tac-tac hellfire warning)
Where waterfall and rowan rush,
Down and up, among the rocks,
On wilderness air of diamond light:
Your steady spirit's eager progress.
What faith is it that brings you back?
What text ordains your April mission
While the hill still wears its bib of snow?

(vi) Grey Wagtail (*Montacilla cinerea*)

for Bernard

First one must stand
Where the heart belongs,
Never missing a beat?
Harder to do than you think?
So I was writing when
You flew into my head:
Another favoured spot
In your varied habitat.

Elusive upstream or in
Grey town square, quietly:
Your wing's exquisite waterline,
Your *nom de plume*, your
Cardiometer tail, blinking,
Where puddle meets sky:
Neither grey nor yellow,
Neither here nor there.

(vii)   Moorhen (*Gallinula chloropus*)

Had I set out to find it or
Known what I had in mind,
That would have been another way
Of looking at it, but it was more
Spontaneous than that or
Undetermined; more like this.

And, to tell the truth, I'm not
Convinced that I can speak of it
At all, in any common sense.
Though I've no problem exclusively
Believing my ears or eyes:
A momentary disturbance

Screened by trees, no different
From any other day in March
I chose to trespass in the wood,
Its rules made for breaking
Like the snap of a twig underfoot,
And found the pond

I never knew was there before
And saw the moorhen brooding,
Its quick bright glance as
Nervous as the pond's surface.
All its eggs in the one basket
Out on a limb like this.

(viii)   Sandpiper (*Actitis hypoleucos*)

Where the valley sags and the stream's
Glacier fritters briefly in a shallow run
Of stones, bog cotton blows and it's soggy
Underfoot, I come upon that place where
The sandpiper once started into flight
Going *twee-eee*, and again *twee-*...
On out of hearing, and stopped the morning
In its tracks, the mountain silenced:
A story of Goliath and the summer snipe.

(ix) Ringed Plover (or Sea-Lark, *Charadrius hiaticula*)

My question this bright shoreland morning is:
Whether without the trailing wing, the plaintive calling,
I'd find what it seeks to distract me from or not?

Or can I gauge I'm getting warmer, boiling even,
As (to turn things on their head) in childhood games of
Hunt-the-thimble, the clamour rises the closer one steps?

Here again it doubles back, in fits and starts, or briefly
Keels over, to up the pathos. I know what its game is.
But what is mine about a plover's nest I failed to find?

(x) Heron (*Ardea cinerea*)

It is impossible to exclude you from the ark of birds,
Though you stand far back in stillness of how many aeons?

However early we must rise to catch you, reflecting
On the flooding world, with tireless gaze.

However few fish there are to go round and however
Unsociable you are. When the waters reach

The topmost spindly branches where you wade on air and flap
Beside your nest, screeching and screaming defiance:

However you make the hair stand up on the backs of our necks
As if we remembered a time when we knew the perils of amphibious life

More intimately, we will lower the boat and row to meet you
Our belled oars labouring in wind and rain.

(xi) Swallow (Y Wennol *Hirundo rustica*)

i.m. R.S. Thomas, d. 25 September 2000

That *when* sound in you migrates to my tongue,
Now you are gone and the sky turns wintry.

We can't say that we saw you leave.
But suddenly the skies are bare and soon the trees.

In any language the word for absence is empty
But of what we need time to tell.

Nothing I know, from the way I'll always see you
Skimming the hay-meadow in westerly light

After however many thousand miles have fallen
To your sickle and still you wheel and dart

Declaring to the skies one makes a spring
Forever, forget summer and winter in the heart.

(xii)   Jay (*Garrulus glandarius*)

A stained glass window glimpsed through a wood?
Speculum of blue, lustrous lattice in your side.

Innocence, my eye. *J* for Judas more like:
Thirty pieces of silver in your stare.

Or d'you think I came down with
The last shower of rain, green as that acorn in your beak?

(xiii)   Chaffinch (*Fringilla coelebs*)

Inching your way, hopping-running,
Among the chaff of the morning's
Bird-table badinage, you call out

Pink-pink, pink to winter's red
-raw sun, the slate-blue wash of sky
Foreboding wild weather in the hedge.

Day's prospects look as slender as you seem,
Little as the light in that frozen
Crystal sliver of a puddle where

You peck at crumbs of frost and tap
The numb stone with your tuning fork.
But pink, you go, with perfect pitch:

Pink-pink to winter's rumbling baritone
And ruddied storm-drift plumage of slate-blue
And tattered blast as you take wing.

(xiv) Pheasant *(Phasianus colchicus)*

Comes under the wall where it's broken, onto the road:
Humble not a word for him, though; nor his gait

In his scaly crocodile party shoes walking
Delicately on his toes like an elderly gent with corns.

But so burnished, Oriental in his princely ornament,
So finely beaten, his dark copperware

Laced like damascene, with the black rim tip
Indent of the craftsman's hammer mottling

His waistcoat-breast. How well he has worn the night
Down all these years, a thousand and one years exiled,

Out late and looking for the way home, his majesty
In all his finery, still dressed for the banquet, at dawn.

(xv) Kestrel *(Falco tinnunculus)*

As if in a startling stoop it had blacked out and
G-force too great to bear sent it hurtling headlong down.
Or the cocktail of toxins in its bloodstream mounted
critically, as the air up there thinned and thinned.
And a mote, a beam, a retinal blur swam in its ultraviolet gaze
tipping out of control the balance of its poise.

She died in the ghost scene working, as she'd have wanted.
How do birds die, naturally? In starving cold…
In sleep benignly, hopping the proverbial twig?
In mid-air, stalling sweetly? This one the larger female
with its wings folded neatly looked like a votive offering
in an ancient cult, a swaddled dead papoose.

Groomed feather-perfect by uprushing air it lay,
cushioned and half-camouflaged by rufous bracken,
in springy tufted grass. So keen to know it at first hand
I stepped into the thicket, to pick it up between
thumb and fingers, across its shoulders.
Youth's touch tentative, failing at first to grasp?

A slight touch, like a trial-run. The touch on the shoulder
you give to rouse someone from sleep. Cautious
not to startle, but in this case not to startle myself,
supposing the thing was taking forty winks and might
start up wildly into flight, threshing light-as-air,
husk from which though flown, as never before the bird would fly.

(xvi)   Magpie *(Pica pica)*

Thief in evening dress at Hawthorn Castle,
what sheen in your coat-tails this draughty April.

Between your raucous hedge–chatter and
effete flight, the swiftness of your eye

deceives the hand, bright as a bride's ring… I
may falter but whether in your spring ceremonials

or at your roadside snacks on the hop, I'd not
dine with the likes of you, save with a long spoon.

(xvii)   House Martin *(Delichon urbica)*

for Alan and Jean Pickering

The house martins made a horse-shoe of
thumb-prints at the peak of our roof
this year, nutshell husks of dried mud.

Each time they rose and darted up so
busily our hopes rose with them
and looked up, as if grown taller with praise.

Then things suddenly came unstuck.
An omen I wondered but for them or us?
They deserted anyway.

The blessing we nearly had: the story of our lives,
hit or miss like their whitewash slapdash
all summer down our neighbour's door.

(xviii)   One for the Road

for Patrick

Visiting my notebook once again,
A notebook smudged and worn:

I find a place where the corncrake still
Goes at it with his sharpening stone

And rusty shears beside the road as if
He has time on his side of the wall.

Bird Scarer

All morning an automatic gun
goes pop... pop... pop... pop...
at steady intervals across the fields.

But the rooks play beggar your neighbour
and settle here to hoe in lines, open and shut,
like collapsible black brollies between showers.

I've thought of buying a gun like that
and hang up my rattle but then
what would I do with my time?

Once or Twice

No water here beyond a netted garden pond
with a slightly worse for wear plastic heron
tilting unconvincingly at leaves on the lawn.

No running stream, no remote tarn, no light
to speak of but suburban grey at bonfire time
in the damp no-man's land between October

and November. Nothing to raise a glance or
prick the heart of a Sunday morning after
the night before. Or so placidly I tell myself.

Then somewhere near a gull scolds suddenly,
out of the grey, just once. Once is enough?
Or not enough? Listen out for more?

Once is enough to give rise to doubt.
Odd to be so suddenly surprised by that.
Twice and you begin to believe your ears?

The mind flies off to some lost mountain tarn
and all the noise of a nesting colony
fills the air wildly, as never heard before.

After which, it all comes round again,
as if it was really there and not a dream.
Though I know precisely twice is impossible

once upon a time's a fraction of the story too.
So I sit here this morning tilting at memory
gazing out upon a netted garden pond

like a slightly worse for wear heron tilting
unconvincingly at lines on a page.
No water here beyond a netted garden pond...

Now, Then

Wake early for an early start and softly
while the world sleeps tight go where

the first of day begins and dawn–light
throws a loop around the nursing air

of some old song you have to heart but
guard well that space between you and

the chorus and only to your self attend:
step up, now then, and sing undaunted.

Rookery Nook

Last night I leant under the backdoor lintel
above the crescent oakwood and listened to
the roosting rooks and jackdaws jostling.

Though you could hardly tell one thing from another
out there, still they cawed and counter-cawed
deafening the village that never hears them.

Just when I thought I'd heard the last of them:
a squawking shade flew out and back again
to settle higher up or lower down the pecking-order.

And once again all hell broke loose. But as at last
it dawned on me what this enquiry might yet entail
I closed the door and left them to it

like abandoning an unfinished poem.
The other line might be to establish when their day begins.
Scrap the whole thing and start again?

But when would I have to rise for that
and could I believe my ears even so,
stood there rubbing my eyes in the bleary doorway?

Set Aside

Look here at how this country's running into life:
as if it's died and gone to heaven.

Up on the hill the pasture plays a five bar blues,
its gate half-hinged hangs jammed wide open.

A hare pricks up his ears and dreams of fisticuffs to come.
The dutch barn's empty and the byre dry as a granary.

A barn-owl's taken on the tenancy,
like a ghost it combs dusk's thistle meadow

and haunts the hedgerows towards dawn. Wheat fields once,
now ghostly in their weeds, look more dead than alive

like someone who came through chemotherapy.
But soon red poppy corpuscles will flood the eye

and tares to warm the cockles of my heart.
And what might that be grating by the road?

Contra Heraclitus

The pool as black as tarmac swims
In thunder rain. The wagtail skims
To feed on insects we can't see
For looking into the beaded downpour.
It hovers and flirts and loops
Beyond the hotel window where
Tourists dine in sorry groups,
And pray tomorrow will be fine.

Meanwhile I try to show I don't belong.
I read my book and take my time,
Glance dispassionately at the rain.
But see how the wiser wagtail knows
To adapt his habits as he goes.
Between the rows of cars, he flits,
And wags, and up he darts to find
His dinner served on number plates.

Back there the shadowed stream,
Its black rocks glistening with rain
And mossy gunk and water-slime,
Pours into a bubble-beaded pool,
Pied itself in dark-light, where up
The wagtail loops, to kiss the air.
Just so nebulous it is but commonplace
To step in the same river twice.

Arboretum

'The subject is very difficult, and the Irish ollaves had no interest in making it plain to outsiders.'

Robert Graves

(i)   Silver Birch (*Betula pendula*)

As if seeded from the Northern Lights
and the ghostly watermarks of wilderness,
haunt of bears and wolves, it stands here
almost too bright to believe, at the year's end,
knee-deep in winter's carnage where
rusted bracken hoards a trove of leaf-mould:
O material light, like a painter's impasto
flaked at the edge of brush- or knife-stroke...

So sight floods to a halt in it and thickens
each forsaking minute with last leavings
drained from December's ditch and sky,
like something almost lost to memory
brought to mind: enough to hold me here,
to see the stars sown early like spring wheat.

(ii)   Heather (*Calluna vulgaris*)

'But white heather is lucky, being a protection against acts of passion.'

Somewhere I remember a sprig of you
preserved in the bottom of a bottle.
A bottle of what? Whisky or purest
peat-water? One and the same, it seemed.

I could see your small springy twist of
timber with its trunk darkened, and
slightly silvered, your scant crown blowing,
like a small tree, in a drystone wall.

I filled my glass, to look further into it,
to see how you had grown there
but though I emptied the bottle
I never did get to the bottom of it.

(iii)   Silver-Fir (*Abies alba*)

'Like a solitary fir tree egoistically separate and pointed upward I stand,
casting no shadow, and only the wood-dove builds its nest in my branches.'

Søren Kierkegaard

For you, like a first-born, I have such tender care it might
prove a curse to you in later life, but not here and now,
in the corner I've cleared for you to bless it with your elegance.

On your label it says you're intolerant of exposure
and pollution and so vulnerable to aphids that
'other species are preferred'. But not my dear by me.

You are the first of them forever in my heart. I note as well
that 'alba' in you and it plays to my folly a loyalty unearned,
truth be told, in a corner, god forbid, of England.

We must all compromise wherever we find ourselves or
wherever we are found wanting some nonsense or other.
So I press my heel round you clockwise, the blunt hours

of my step measure how far I am from home. What goes around
comes around they say. There is nowhere to walk straight to.
Not even where you stand, the solitary fir tree.

(iv) Furze (Gorse or Whin, *Ulex europæus*)

Easy to make new meaning of it on this bluff outcrop now
my heart's headland with its fool's gold in purse upon purse
of sharp memories, childish memories, where I came in youth,
as I come now in my parallel universe, always parallel
now, to sort my head out, when the world below had turned
the binoculars round the right way on my spendthrift
kicking against the pricks and the tall furze boxed my ears
and stung my cheeks with sharper than sharp scratches and stabs
as I struggled up to sulk above the little seaboard town.

They burn gorse back don't they? And its smoke blows across
the hills leaving the slopes black the better to grow
green again, for the grass to have its day too, before
the spikes themselves spread their crackling fire and
flower and flower without season until they are also
back where they used to be, pricking and scratching
their welcome, warming the heart of the worst winter,
growing again and getting back above themselves:
funny goblin heads wagging on the tearaway wind.

They're enough at nightfall to startle even the least superstitious child.
What's the price of a jerry-can of blue paraffin and a light
to catch it on a spring morning? The furze being ill-behaved until
he is subdued at the vernal equinox? Never too high?
So here I kindle you prickly pride, yet again, as if for the first time,
and scorch you back to the last page, to the last line,
to the last gorse-bird's song, the last gorse-chat, gorse-hatch,
-hatcher, -thatcher: whinchat, stonechat, wheatear, linnet's
growing back through my poems in my parallel furze-bush universe.

(v)   Rowan (*Sorbus aucuparia*)

No doubt but your one foot holds
all hope there is for you,
high in that cleft of shadow–substance
where the ouzel sings to the torrent's dance.

So I remember and am attached to you
and that bird, earthed to the voltage of its song,
as I stand uprooted, in this suburban garden,
a hand on one of you, to curse my luck.

(vi)   Ash (*Fraxinus excelsior*)

You're cold as the east wind this morning but I lean in to you
and huddle here for shelter as if those black pyramidal points

at your branch tips rattling the day's skylight still hold heat
in their embers and the spirit of spring is already jetting

invisibly to ignite April with your slender flowers. They say
your roots run down as deep as your branches reach skyward.

I have read how the first branch of a maiden ash might
cure all ills and who am I in middle life in middle England

this winter's morning now to doubt it? All balancing acts require
at least an element of faith. So with the squall's passing I

gamely swing my stick and prod the road for home, desperately
trying to remember every ash I've known and every April wood.

(vii)   Hawthorn (*Crataegus monogyna*)

So hedged about as you are with omens and
legends, how can I ever hope to break through,
to see you unburdened of everything, except
spring blossom or starkly criss-crossed winter light,
when your Christ's crown, your May catalogue
of antiseptic bridal wear, become you so well?
And your Lear-on-the-heath bad-hair-day blows
my mind to see you in the cold blast blown? Or
I feel I've stared too hard into a Jackson Pollock
and thrown a fit and found myself coming to
on the dark side of a late Beethoven quartet,
played on a seventy-eight, with one of your thorns
for a needle, as I've heard said can be done?
How on earth can I ever hope to see you,
wood for trees if not timber for timbre? Well,
in two successive gardens now, I've planted
you and nurtured, and entered into your being,
like a wren or a robin or sudden song-thrush
going in and out, unscathed, or briefly singing,
and stood to savour you, at all points of the
thorny compass, in blossom and fruit and leaf-fall.
And as you know there are evenings when I've
softly closed my hand about your shank, and
stirred you round and round, as I've been told
will radiate down to the outposts of your root-tree
and give them firmer hold in the underworld,
and never harm came of it, not a scratch, nor
a penny the poorer have I been, but *au contraire*
I've thrived and revelled in your beauty.

(viii)   Briar (*Rubus fruticosus*)

The ways of the world are as involved and
barbed as this entanglement I'm wading in
to pick blackberries, stepping on the coiling waves.

But if only life could be as simple and rewarding in
its punishments, pricks and snares. Here, too, one thing
leads to another, until you're in it up to your neck.

There's no easy way back either when it starts to rain
and it rains harder, until you're drowning.
Every time you reach to pick it's like

a swimmer's wild stroke must be your last but no
there's still more to be had. So avidly, I fill
my plastic ice-cream box of pleasure to the lid.

(ix)   Hazel (*Corylus avellana*)

This is where to take time and make it run
divinely as the light that leaps here:

where the jay lurks and the pheasant
picks his progress at the wood's border

and the thrush divines song in the air, song
everywhere… as far back as you can remember

its forked beak flickering like a snake's tongue,
so rapidly the toothed leaves seem to shiver for joy

but it's sudden spring rain that shakes them
and spots the thrush's breast with slanting drops.

As if Ovid wrote this poem when you were young,
a mere sapling yourself and hazel-eyed.

(x) Ivy (*Hedera helix*)

Be silent unless you have something
better than silence to say.

(xi)   Oak (*Quercus robur*)

Put the wood in the hole: there's a draught
through here like the north wind itself.

The draft of a poem on the poetry of fire-gazing:
scrunched in your embers and going up in smoke

up through your trunk's black chimney where
a crowd of poems might shelter from the axe

blown away to the acorn stars from which
the tall dreams grow. I can hear it all in this still hearth.

To think: there are poems have lived a thousand years
and strike like lightning even now.

(xii)   Holly (*Ilex aquifolium*)

Whoever worked to cut the template for your leaves
pricked his finger, as you know, and drew a bead of blood.

He was rehearsing for the greater project of the stars:
his life's work, you might be tempted to suppose.

But believe me, it's the same old story: the best effects
arrive as if from nowhere in the mind the mind has been before.

Truth stands where it is seeded. As here at the wood's border
your crown at evening holds against the sky the first stars I ever saw.

(xiii)   Dwarf Elder (*Aegopodium podagraria*)

My heart goes out to you, even now,
as I turn on you my tenacious spade.
A lesser shrub but lettered and inclined
to spread, shade from the scary days of
human sacrifice. I remember well at least
the cover you lent my own dire deeds.

As with the *Diana .177* (aged 8 or 9) I'd
skulk all afternoon in your pungent world,
ready to slug it out with anything that moved,
compiling an alphabet of small dead birds,
Blackie to Wren, would have us both arraigned
at The Hague were there justice in the world.

(xiv)   White Poplar (*Populus alba*)

Today, October turns and turns
your shoals dark and light, in a flood of air.
The rain blowing from you reminds me
of the showers of pollen a season ago
that filled the air to gasping for air.

The wind runs and runs and the leaves
cannot quicken any longer in your branches
so fly faster through the rain's fine spray,
blown along the air like giant pollen
in flurries, the air itself gasping for air.

The tree of old age, they say. But even
Hercules might die today for want of breath,
staring at aspens through a windswept window.
Not everyone can say they own trees,
said the old man suddenly, in revelation.

Yesterday he'd struggled on his stick
and dragged a plastic chair a hundred yards
the better to survey them, breathless
on a day of such autumnal stillness
not a leaf stirred or fell to earth.

(xv)   Alder (*Alnus glutinosa*)

What on earth were you in the other life?
Something the river has forgotten and keeps looking for?

Like water off a duck's back. Like the last light of day or
the last shadow of morning, before the moorhen mops it up.

Like the original formula for waterproof.
Like the world before the flood. The jetty on the Styx.

The sunken causeway home. The resurrection and the light.
Read your lips? Your lips are sealed. Let the wind whistle

through you, as if in the know, and your dipping branch scribble
its ancient script in the gleaming water from here to eternity.

(xvi)   Willow (*Salix viminalis*)

'Burn not the willow, a tree sacred to poets.'

Beware the soft hand-shake. It is
the mark of one whose mind is elsewhere.

A supple heart is strongest of all
for weaving withies into fish-traps.

Ancient sayings from the poetics
of the workshop for the blind.

(xvii)   Elder (*Sambucus nigra*)

Your crooked timber's brittle but pithy
like a commentary on the aesthetic.

You sidle at the outhouse corner,
digging in a drain for a living.

Judas with his noose chose you:
once in bad company, always a sinner.

You stink in the nostrils of the righteous wood.
Like any outcast it's neglect fosters you.

One day we'll come along and casually
take you out, ripping a saw through you

like the wretched of the earth anywhere,
no matter your literature is extensive.

No matter your blossom intoxicates summer and
your dark fruit lights winter to its doom.

(xviii)   Yew (*Taxus baccata*)

But what a pretext for reflection this,
a mouthpiece for the dead, a root to each
pair of lips. In the old lore 'yew' and 'I'
both stood for death, you know? Death,
then, is evergreen and in the pink, as in
your strong and supple limbs, your
darkest leaves and small red fruit, with which
you've cast a shadow for so long across
this limestone corner of the countryside.

For what? To assist us in our melancholy?
Or just so that a skulking blackbird might
pause to sit and gaze a thousand years
while you bring light to dark like this and
dark to light your silence with his song?

Headland

for Michael

Migration of gorse over thirty summers:
A linnet's flight between
Two stars of outcrop karst.
Can you say you saw it?
A lifetime in an instant
Wherever thought runs here.

I remember when those golden purses
Blew my heart as far as Môna's isle
And every feeling soared
On tugging-hugging woollen air,
The seaborne day delayed
However tides ran there.

Things held by the eye, where
Gentians grew, or pipits nested,
And in the mind's eye too:
The year's doomed youth
Who lost his hold and fell,
Overreaching for an egg.

Belonging

Who put the longing into it?
The longing to leave so that
We might belong in longing
To return again, and again?

Who put the being into it?
The being that is never the same
So that when we come back to it
All we have is a name?

Allt

Lines from an Autobiography

All through the night the tide
roared on the air, roared in
the trees and soughed about
our steady stone-built, slate
-roofed house, *Tan-yr-allt*
'under the wooded hill':
where we slept in the roof
as near heaven as we could
though not as near the stars
as the wild *allt* itself but
in middle-earth above the coast,
borderers in every sense
(M^cs not aps), between sea
and mountain, sleeping dream
and waking, under the
foundering air: all through
the night, *ar hyd yr nos.*

Ar lan y môr… Not just dreams
either but faith also, though of
no formal kind for us. When they
sang in that school hall 'There is
a Green Hill Far Away…' my
clock-watching mind's eye
saw no Christ but Eden's
wind-bent bluff blowing
gorse and hawthorn, larch
-scrub in limestone outcrop,
nestling violets, gentians, cowslips,
every kind of bird and
springtime egg, jackdaws
cackling, ravens going *cronk*
and back-vowelled gulls
bobbling and keening, guttural
fulmars, all riding high as
hope above the town.

And sitting here idling at six
of a morning (in Massachusetts),
my head spins as if years were
altitude and all my travails had been
to climb them, and find myself
turned inside-*allt* again, clinging
by my fingertips, reaching for
a gull's egg breakfast...
As if I might begin to make
meaning of my lot now in that
cold morning then, above the
town, summer coming in
(as now) from England's last
satanic mills, for donkey-rides,
punch and crocodile, deck-chairs
between downfall... Happy Valley.
Whistling in the dark until
autumn shut up shop and
banged and rattled into winter.

And left us to it, as I'm left to it
here, haunted by that place:
whistling in the dawn, scribbling
to make sense of those gaping
wide-eyed days, yielding and
unyielding. Still unfallen,
I never looked down on
anything then, but looked both
down and up, longing from
that fastness, atop a lane as
rocky as a mountain (mind's
rough road to climb again).
And looked away from lessons
and the law, back into my
heart's dark wood, distracted
as I grew, and grew weary
and wary to embrace expulsion,
already by then pen-in-hand,
digging word-bait, hooking bass...

A tale since washed overboard,
writing the lives of fish, and birds:
I spy with my little eye something
beginning… as I strode out at ten
-years-old, *TUF*-booted then hobnailed,
lost and found, under the high
Carneddau… from first of March
to the last of September, fishing;
at sixteen fingered by the poets
and fatefully fired into orbit
like Sputnik over Snowdonia
by Thomas & Thomas & Co.,
Graves, Hopkins, MacDiarmid,
Lawrence, Kavanagh, Synge…
whirled slowly round their wheeling
word-warp rhyme-realm, until,
one November drunk and
sober I made my re-entry
and fell to earth on Inis Mór.

And stayed there and felt
at home in that limestone
landscape, sea-rocked at
the edge of the world,
though scarce a tree to be heard there
but the sound of a tumultuous wood
heard everywhere, at sea in the
driftwood flotsam-jetsam
deciduous Atlantic…

Our *allt* was no Eden like that,
but a once-formal garden, then
wilderness: corner of a small estate
that fell to us, the villa of some
Roman (captain hotelier) run to
ruin and rendered barbarous,
preferred above humbler Coed Coch.
We occupied his gardener's lodge
and lived walled off from Rome,
not citizens and, if natives, not
descendants but outsiders.

Behind high walls topped with
valerian: rabbits in the nettles,
geese one time beneath the wood
stood sentry at the western gates,
cats gone feral, foxes for wolves;
a sundial that told no time in
Roman numerals, and honey
in the hive, a vinery under glass
with antique iron heating ducts
(deep tanks, one sunken, like
a Roman bath unearthed) in rack
and ruin, though bearing fruit,
grapes for a Welsh elegy, drunk
under towering nordic pines
that swayed and staggered overhead
dizzying the windswept stars,
their cones clustered stars.

They stood in phalanxes above
the courtyard and up the side of
Fferm like props on the frontier
in a movie called 'The Last Days
of Marcus Aurelius'. And yet
in summer-light those trees
were pure Mediterranean: their
trunks, oyster-shell edged, orange-
pink-grey, impossible pastels, black
damascene lace-maps. Their cones
clicked open in the heat or
clattered down (our winter kindling)
to rest on beds of needles and
grasses where grasshoppers
hopped and thrushes bathed in
dust and tawny shafts of sun.

Allt… one of the oldest words,
older than any English word?
(But halt and prick your ears
along the marches to hear *holt*.)
And young now on every native
childhood's tongue, almost as though

Rome had never been or England's
empty empire. At John Bright
Grammar School (neither *ysgol* nor
radical but patronising pseudo-
Arnoldian), we did not learn and
learnt the lie of the land. What
the eye doesn't see the heart
can't grieve over, and we didn't
grieve, nor do I now. But what
wonders in that wild place the
heart might miss a beat to tell.

Each morning as I brushed my teeth
I looked out on Bryn Maelgwyn,
bardic *allt*, on Llanrhos and Deganwi:
landmarks in the *Mabinogi* where
pouting Taliesin sang and *blerwm,*
blerwm babbled back his rivals
blerwm, blerwm... Barbaric Welsh
to Roman ears, to Latin ears and
Anglo-Saxon: *allt* where I skulked,
the mind's *allt* to which those
reticent hicks called Prytherch,
Llewelyn and ap Rhys Owen
retreated, biding their time, cannily
keeping their counsel in the
dark wood of their tongue.

M^c maybe I am but what ish
my nation? I was born there...
Yet no man, as Taliesin said,
sees what supports him. So
soon I went, eager to leave
and not incapable of leaving.
Though back I came within a year:
O dark wood, O *allt* unaltered,
to leave, and leave again for home
(from America, the short way now).

Croeso

for Justin McNeillie

As well try to steer by the tattered constellations
as by memory or its ghostly prompters where
the lanes in this back country meet.

There's no going back, quite literally.
You'd end up in a ditch like a grave, listening to owls,
star-gazing to the nearest phone wherever that might be

there being no signal here either. But I'd go back
all right on the conceit that led me into this
not half an hour from where I want to be I swear.

I'd unwind the whole thing as far as it goes
and start again and know I was well off
waiting at the road end for someone to arrive.

After Taliesin

I've been:

The raven from the ark, flying to and fro.
A curragh in the wild Atlantic.
A corncrake crexing loud in spring.
A Guinness tide.
A drowned man's eyes.
The spit of seals.
A dab hand.
A poet to the *Naomh Eanna*.
A blackbird's song at evening.
A stone of skate.
A whaup.
A descendant of Rheged.
A pierhead light.
A wage-slave in middle England.
A galaxy in the pine-wood's racing tide.
Not a pair of pampooties.
A playboy.
A hook in the mouth of a fish.
A waking dream: a proud father.
A thorn in my own side.
A hand in my own downfall.
The grin on the cormorant's face.
A hand of mackerel.
A star at dawn.
The light in stone.
A fool to myself.
The traveller hurrying through the evening.

In Vino Veritas

The wires ran straight
like a stave to hold a tune in line.

But the vine wove its own
design as if to prove it could.

With leafy grace notes and trilling
tendrils it composed itself.

So learn how to hold your drink
and find your own way home.

Hare

To start a hare? So still, the eve of March,
I'm led to ask, has your heart stopped like mine?
Form and meaning so snug together.

At Roundstone

for Tim Robinson

At Roundstone the tide was in,
making its peace with the moon.
Night clambered aboard and the air
filled with sea-sound and bird-cry,
as if making headway for... let's not
say where: but the heart knows its
harbour, registered there and still
fishing, with torn net and star-haul
blowing bright as the March light
that we stopped en route to stalk
to its source, down a bay of coral
whose name I've forgotten, vanishing
in the biting wind that blew there,
before we made it darkling to your board.
And you and I and Máiréad had
only to smile and laugh on meeting,
like long-lost comrades (or a conclave
of corncrakes, grinning), so much had
that island meant, looked for
and unlooked for, every square inch
of the heart, beyond measure.
But all we ever wanted is meaning,
to note the finest nuances of stone
and light and how they map
themselves and map us. For meaning
regarded as an end of desire,
as another island-haunter said,
is value, as found, for example,
in the hypnosis of repetitive days
(your phrase), and must itself be
charted, fractal by fractal, and
converted word for word, minutely
into words, page by Lilliputian page,
to show what this world has endured
and lost, and would have lost
the more (time out of mind)

but for your finding your vocation
ever to hand around stone and sea
unfolding and folding landscapes.

American Wake

Heading for America, on St Stephen's evening,
A vision from below swam up to haunt me:
The islands in the bay's mouth, gliding.
The day was turning thin, no sign of habitation,
From that height, or hint of coloration, yet
From the cast of light I knew, if one asked there,
'Will it rain?', the question was her answer.
It seemed a miracle to me that I should see them:

I never take a window seat (to speed escape
On landing) but stood up just to stretch my legs,
And by some gift or grace of timing, glimpsed
Them, through a port-hole: the parting glass,
Raised between us, and since who must go, and who
Must stay? the moment made me wonder.

From Another World

Kilmurvey in March 1969, suddenly remembered

for Duncan Wu

Maybe that rock and those strange people were
The figure for his trusted truth, his ariel soul,
Blown to that shore, the depth and inwardness he craved?
Certainly, even for someone of his age and time,
He took the longer way, to face, and not to face,
The world; but better that than staying home?
Home at that age was nondescript and bored:
An empire in decline now turned upon its kind,
Murderous to protect a parasitic pound.
Time crumbled in his hand: still Caesar kept command.

But here was a world in which his soul might flit
As goldfinches looped round and round their
Rocky ownership. Cuckoo, swallow, crex, were
Annual guests and stayed in mind as signs and wonders.
But truly for him, ever, to lead a life like those people?
The vagrant species is a sport, without meaning,
Rhyme or reason: common there but
Here bizarre, beyond their naming, like
The one that morning, tugged by the wind
And fluttering at the shoreline for a moment:

A shadow's shade back from the dead? A haunting
From another world. What was it? Briefly
Dabbling, windswept there? How it blew in
An astral freak, a miracle time won't repeat,
An alienation effect, a Duchamp by Audubon,
Like the weather of those days we package as
The Sixties now: a freak decade, of fugitives,
Or losers, take your pick, dodging the universal
Draft, a rampant old guard's call to fall in line.
The whole thing, like that freak storm, blew his mind.

Smogairle Rōin

(Irish for jellyfish: spit of the seal)

Judging from the sea that day
some of them had gone down

overnight with summer colds.
Others still worse off

coughed up their lungs like
smokers, leaving long trails

of rusty phlegm and snot
as thick as blubber.

Là-bas

Those days when we were beaten back
to wile away the remnants of a storm
around the sinks and basins of the port
I went, blowing my hands to warm my heart,
and *C'est bien ça*... the Frenchman called
down from *La Roche* of Bordeaux, as if
down memory, like a poet's ghost, *là-bas*...

Then in some harbour bar *l'étranger*, I waited,
the *longue durée noire* of Guinness and chips,
until midnight now ready, salted at the door,
topped up the weather's glass, but sank me,
my un-mercurial wits, in submarine depths
of unchanged sheets, at the Hôtel de la Mer-
de... to meet the morning wrecked divinely.

Water Table

At the heritage centre the curator asked
'Did it rain much in your time?'
'Heavy rain?' he persisted, 'In sheets,
rushing off the rocks?' It rained, I said,
smiling, it rained all right, week on end,
in at the front door out by the back.
'But did the water ever rise up?'
He gestured with a sweep of his hand,
indicating the ground beyond.
I shrugged. 'Well I'll tell you,' he said,
'Last December, in a sudden flood
it rose two feet beyond in that hollow…'
I marvelled. 'It will happen again,'
he said, 'no doubt. It's only a matter of time.'
I looked at the sky on the hill.
'And you know how I know?'
he demanded. 'I'll tell you. There,
d'you see? in that little hut, there's a table,
all under lock and key, and it tipped that table,
would you believe? …I know because
on the table there was a book, a ledger
for noting the numbers of visitors passing.
Now, that book was wet…
Its pages all wrinkled and curled.
You mark my words…' I marked them.

Meditation in Homage to the Playboy

for Antony Farrell

How can it be that what I keep coming down to is
a mere toehold, once again, in a story of my own making,
whose plot I enacted when I was little more than twenty?
I look into this old photo of him, and I'm swimming,
drunkenly out of my depth, my belonging tenuous, like a father
who's trespassed where he no longer has any business, but
possibly to be forgiven, if he's lucky, to tell the truth,
to this youth leaning in an island doorway, posing with a tea-cup,
hand in pocket, looking away, stage left.

Wouldn't any of the more modest stories have done as well instead?
Not that they didn't obtrude their guilt-edged reproaches. For a time;
and mockery, for years: wise before and after the event,
we told you so, but would you listen? Fool! In view of which it's not
so very hard to say I owe everything to him, his sense of timing
and value, his extraordinary absence of interest in money? His
fuck you? And now that we begin to prove each other true,
not in belonging but believing is where sense begins?
That beginning word, singing siren on the rocks.

In the beginning was the sentence ravelled towards death.
How many pages long before it wrecks? How many copulas? How many
changes of tense and subject? And how many ruses to postpone like
Scheherazade the last word, because in the end we must always be always
one jump ahead? So round and round the rock the ragged rascal runs. But
believe me, peace of mind is the last thing anybody wants.
That's something I had from the horse's mouth. Is that why he
doesn't look the camera in the eye? He knows the truth, that all we need
is faith enough to put at risk the air we breathe, and light of day.

Which seems just outlandish to say as it was to embark that wild winter.
Is it my comfort or my problem that I know what lies in the direction
he is looking? (While at his back the whole romantic tradition
stumbles over the crags like Frankenstein? And the skylarks hit the roof
and the poor plod on preferring life at least to death, given a choice?)
He never believed in either/or's stark simplicity but always also
unspokenly in beauty, as being the more human path not falsely drawn,
and that surprises me to say, but it is true. Daydreaming along
with *Six Existentialist Thinkers* in his pocket, he might have known it too.

But I can tell you he's not looking at anything in particular,
not at the passage of a bird between the gardens, it being spring,
or anything like that. He's more vacant this brief vagrant,
and certain possibly of just one thing, that vagrancy and vacancy have
enough in common and enough at odds for interest to accrue
between them, like poems. He stashed it away for me, as if there was
no tomorrow, and only tomorrow. Is there nothing else? Is there anything
else but where I make those beginnings come round now? A future not
mouthing platitudes, or rehearsing how to bring things to a close?

Cimetière Marin

Tombs on the headland, dull with cold,
Rise in the groundswell ahead, like seals inspecting
The upper world, souls of the drowned, they say.

Their backs grey-black, their flanks mottled
And starred with lichen, they ride it out there,
As if waiting for the tide to hoist them higher.

The Outbuilding

I do not need to be doing this at all, but once again
I wander off to make them happy and inspect
the outbuilding. Such places haunt the elderly
as they recede. Now neither has the strength to
walk here, still less to make the bottom of the door
judder its first steps up onto its hinges.

And I am thinking how next spring we'll have
to take the roof in hand and fix a leaky window.
I come only for their peace of mind. I know
already how things stand, cobwebbed together
at the corners, patched and mended, cobbled once
in the daily makeshift of more vigorous times.

I remember, I forget. The sum of things is like that. Shockingly,
I imagine, in their minds, the same spores advancing
that here subdue the creosote can and bandage it with
gauze, where the leaning scythe looks as if it's had
a stroke, or else is very sad, its mouth turned down
at one corner. How it lost its other leg, don't ask.

Where have you felt anything as cold as metal?
Or smelt that hard dank, somehow angular smell
of iron? Old machinery doesn't die it only fades away.
What am I to do? Put the clock back? Rejuvenate
the tractor? I hover idly looking in, while at my back
the evening light rehearses its farewell.

Lepus

Like Chinese whispers at court, the constellations:
for example, *Lepus*, the hare.

Could I go back I might correct the mishap
that led me such a dance.

All might become as clear as day. But here
the puzzle is I must believe your ears?

Ploughs

We wheel with the gulls.

We weep clods.

We toil between harvests.

We lounge among nettles.

We do not keep our nose clean.

The Blacksmith's Order Centenary

An elegy in memory of John McNeillie 1865–1941 and of
John McNeillie 1916–2002, to be read aloud

From Clarksburn Smithy, Portwilliam, to Mr John McCallam, Clachaneasy, Newton Stewart

> *Sir please Send me acknowledgement*
> *of Scrap Mettel, supplied to you I sent off*
> *on November 30th and also the balance*
> *or whatever it may be until we have*
> *the account squared up as I want that done*
> *until I get my order sent in for some*
> *plough mettels this year in time and*
> *also send me price of what you can*
> *supply plough Boards and soles and*
> *landsides per cwt for this season*
> *I want to make a little alteration on*
> *my patterson plough Broad this year*
> *and You will oblige   John McNeillie*

O I would oblige you, John McNeillie,
hammering at my key Broad here
(the thing we call spellchecker fails)
thinking of your soles and landsides,
your plough mettels... (Microsoft
furrows underneath in red: 'landsides'
and 'mettels'), and that little alteration,
as who would not make if he could?
And see us meet the day on 22 July,
a hundred years away from here, or there,
at nettle-deep rusty Clarksburn Smithy,
this very summer, as it would be? And
what might we not say, by the cwt, together?
(I've often dreamt... and dream still.)
How little future there is in any thing?
And you would know who built to last.
What past the world might care to know?
Technologies of how to make a plough
Broad, patterson or no, or word-processor?

Who said the plough is immortal?

The constellations are as far from me as you,
their sparks hanging fire in God's ruined smithy.
But in your house my father grew,
and we are close, as he was close to you.
And when I look him in his eye it is
an eye you looked into, and when I shake
his hand a hand you shook and shook
a blackened smithy with your clout until
sparks flew like gulls behind a plough
(as Darwin drew). As words would fly,
if I could strike things right, until we had
the account 'squared up', whatever it may be.

And that still shakes me through: that
little span we might have closed, handful
of years to weigh against your mettel. There's
scrap here too in my 'waste bin' by the ton.
So now I toil and sweat to melt it down
and hammer out lines, in your memory,
rugged enough for any rocky road.
I've longed for such a meeting since a boy,
in some hereafter where we might be 'men':
the old man, you, and me, together…
with a bottle of Bladnoch to hand…
Little I thought to hear from you by letter
but here I find you folded neat inside
an envelope, roughly 5 × 3.5, addressed to
Clachaneasy, and sent it seems by hand,
to 'The Crown Implement Works' or
so you scrawled, on 22 July 1901,
regarding yours of 30 November.

Here fog billows down the Bladnoch,
my hand slips… my glass briefly
out of kilter with my lips, and Bladnoch
in her meadows grows sombre like the Styx.

Time never deals in sentiment: it doesn't give a damn
for little alterations or the balance of our lives
or witness or... any of our loyalties (or dis-)...
but from Dis to Disneyworld and farther,
to you and to that other John I'll drink
however much it takes to loose a tongue,
so we might lose and find ourselves again.
At some belated date somehow our tribe
moved from the iron age to the age of scribe,
blacksmith to wordsmith, mettel to paper.
God knows how. Except by 'God' himself,
read in the Bible; and story-telling at your hearth:
of rackrenter Maxwell, and 'mighty men'
of Mochrum, McFee some Irish kin of ours...
tales from the forge, politics of the smithy,
and those books you bought at house sales.
Rabbie Burns, kenned inside oot, and...
Dryden's Virgil? You a man believed in
devil's imps and fairies (Brownyis and
Bogillis), your life closer to 'Tam O'
Shanter', ever than to me? Your labour
never any kind of 'eclogue', Virgilian or other?

Dryden? The one the old man cut his teeth on:
half-schooled first ever writing John McNeillie,
on whom you doted, your pride the prodigy,
author of 'harum-scarum' *Wigtown Ploughman*,
quoted, for all its scandalous swearing, from
the pulpit in the churches of Wigtown,
Portpatrick, Kirkmaiden, Mochrum, Sorbie...
that boy who 'ran about half naked'
now 'shure to do some good to others'?
For that is where he 'shone in waking up
and showing the publick, the houses
and conditions people lives in... the unwashed
ploughmen tribe, born of Divels imps or
poison wasps, led by the divel himself...
cot folks without education or caracter,
only lives for day, and daily bread, and
a fight or a quarl, after thay have thair
bely full, and gets thair tail up...' I quote

your letters at you as you wrote, in English,
though you lived and thought in Scots.

Word-shod together we'll wear longest of all?
So I'll melt your words into my own
and speak on paper as to the first I meet:
just as you told a story... Until I find you
past your last winter, and Hitler rampant:
'let him spin the rope that will hang him'
the end of a tow 'the safest place for a madman',
his ploughshares turned to bombs and tanks;
and you write 'Dear John a few lines to say'
how the world was all that time away,
last lines from you, last from your hand,
amen (I quote from your distress to reap
what comfort?) '...now getting scarce of fodder,
trashed out the last stack and now only two
small stacks of hay, and no sign of grass.
So we are almost on the verge of want,
and money cant get it, so thare we are,
coming on to starvation with losing half
of the turnips with the frost and snow...'
                                    22 July 2001

Father and Son

There's strength in silence, he said,
Looking across at me for emphasis.
The more you say the more malleable
You become. I slipped out on some
Excuse and wrote it down. We'd whisky
In us and my heart foresaw a poem.

Then I sat there gazing, as if through
A window, glazed by the dram. And the view
Stayed me, and I sat silent. And,
If you tell your offspring, he resumed,
Your grandchildren, anything about them:
Tell them what good men they were.

Whose reputation and for what
Are we weighing here, my heart
Faltered? But firmly now,
As if by calculation to forestall…
He gestured at the anaesthetic, and
So I poured and we both drank.

One More Time

By now his outdoor orbits of the house
approach the frequency of comets passing.

Yet when I ask what he's been up to since
he says he's been out in the fields walking.

And at once I know where he means. He says
he goes to keep his mind from wandering.

The Way to Work

You wouldn't start from here?
You can choose where?
To begin where you are not
to get back to where you are?
Pitfalls marked on the map
prove for sure to be the trap.

Time runs backwards. Is that so?
There were visitations as he drove.
He counted them: yellow-hammers...
not since a boy. All that, but where
he wished to get to wasn't there.
The mirror showed the way ahead?

Is it the story of our lives not
to know fate until too late? Not
to know time's clockwise course
is not in forward but reverse,
on the steep hill up, the winding way
to Knowledge and back?

What's this about, you wonder?
Notes made in lay-bys, pulling over,
taking the long way round, slowly.
Compliant traveller too ready
to procrastinate. Too ready to
observe the woodies down for grit

with collars open, dimly lit
under the chestnut candelabra.
It's early but it feels like late.
I'd make it later if I could,
outstay the day on this long road
and never arrive in time.

Weather Permitting

Who hasn't stepped into its world, happening on
small bays along a rocky shore? The tide in
the affairs of no one, take it or leave it, and stood
and stared and listened to small notes of rapid
to-fro birds, against its backwash backdrop, surge
and swell, inhale and exhale, breathe deeply in
the ozone light so strong upon the thumbnail sand
it makes you shield your eyes, your ears full
of sea-sound of all sizes. And what is it for?
Pointless I'd say except that is itself the point.
This cool bright harvest threshed and threshed
like grain or goldrush, panned and panned again,
to no avail. And here and there a little plank,
stamped with the initials of a fishing co-op, cork,
a strand of bright blue nylon rope, convolvulus
of weed and orange line, a bevelled branch
or other crooked lump of wood, trunk and head
of some hardy swimmer's ghost, propped there
on its elbow to watch the running tide all afternoon,
and a pool beside a gloomy rock, islanded in
another world. For heaven's sake? It's not
for anything or anyone, we know. It is what it is.
No point of embarkation or looked-for landing.
Yet when we ask what we will do tomorrow
we both agree at once to bring our picnic here,
weather permitting and the heavens don't open.

Harbourage

They come and go. The light never quite dies out,
kept alive, like hope on life support, starboard and port,
steering them home, staring ahead, the drowned
in their wake, the fortunate stars above, singing
we are the resurrection and the life. Only the weather
rages. What grudge or grievance as to this
ever seemed worth its costly keep? So hope waits
to board and sail and something in becoming
already is, like the dying fall. I find my mind
drifts, and swings round at its mooring, here
on Sunday's sofa, swung round before the set.
Soon I'm elsewhere too, just like them,
in no time. And like them too I repeat myself,
dreaming at the jetty, back to the wall. Where they're
also agitated at the prospect of farewell, or greeting:
count on it that he caught his sailing, got home
safely (please to phone), while I wonder just what
he might unpack next, when he wakes from absence
of how many years, hours or moments, a lifetime away.
We'll talk suddenly and laugh, and sink again…

Then she's one I'll not forget, either. Though I
hardly knew her, come home to die. How long
she'd live uncertain, the summer perhaps, or
just to the march of spring, with its hopefulness
irrepressibly mounting, like the tide, as if for
a better view of the ferry coming at last. And
the young, willing them to hurry disembarking,
so to let them board and be gone, to feel
the giddy world shift at their feet, like sex, and home
so keen-sighted finally fall from its vantage point.
When I do this it is as if footage at the Styx,
always slippery, were suddenly rewound. Until,
I fancy, that one called them to cast their net
on the other side. But devil may care they know
wrong from right. Kick up your heels, sweet boat,
and we will follow suit, their hearts say and
their eyes talk. When we look out to search the

horizon we may fancy we're engaged in descrying
the future or be thankful we cannot know what it will be.

Yet here it is already among us, like Christ
among his disciples, like the light bounding in
the sea-air, bound for the ends of the earth,
of the western world at least (Jesus Christ!)
reflected by a myriad means. But the machine's
fixed relentlessly on forward, steady as we go,
look back as you like. As I do now, to that day again
and see the old man, not old at all but young,
full of vigour in life's rough throng, descending
the gangway, and he hasn't known me for
my wilderness beard – disciple of what faith? – until
I step and tug his sleeve and still, for a split second,
he wonders who it is, touting or begging, some
poor fool? Not as now I see him sat chin down,
or suddenly startled awake, try as I might not to.
Then he steps up for me to offer him my arm,
en route to the loo, unsteady, as if in truth we were
on board and heading for Hades, the waters wrecked
by a sudden squall. Much remains unchanged, yet
everything is different. Keep watch with me,
harbouring heart, with all your perishable freight
this afternoon. The weather seems always to be bad
these days. Yet here's a break might see us still
keep hope alive, wherever we will, the ferry
frisking in the immortal rain and the young,
come by to take his hand and kiss his brow.

The Invective

In homage to Alasdair, mac Mhaighstir Alasdair (c.1698–c.1770)

To know how to curse is to know how to bless.
They are two sides of the same sharp reality.
Should the day dawn when a new whisky's distilled
at Ardnamurchan, let them call it, in your memory,
'The Invective', with the maker's advice on the label:
best knocked back, uncivilly, at daybreak, leaning
in an island doorway, lingering there long enough
to savour the after-taste of laughter, in its scorn
for human frailty and the vanity of poets.

Piss

'He gave it the worst look he had left.'
John Berryman

A man must do more than come from somewhere,
sing the songs of his people and relate their stories

to warrant respect, still less earn praise: I'm bored by
the bravura bores parading their lack on their sleeve.

Their claim that where they come from it's pronounced
to sound like loss is neither here nor there to me.

I piss on their empty pride. I piss on their loss,
their folk measures, their hearty reminiscence and

sneering or sensitive superiority of demeanour, their
transparent manoeuvres to attract the limelight, and I piss

on the dupes who would atone for their want of purity of being
by seeking to sample the nostalgia that dare not speak its home.

I spit in their eyes for shysters. I piss in their repertoire.
I piss down their tin whistles and into their fiddles.

I fill the bladders of their bagpipes with the urine of bevies
of bevies of heavies and echter than echt drams.

I revile them for I know where they come from and why
they lack attention there, and how, should they dare

or presume to return, the locals will soon clip their wings,
cut short their tedious reminiscence, with sharp recollection of their own

(piss on them too). Which is why the bastards won't go home.
But still the call resounds, 'Have you no homes to go to?'

Crying in the Wilderness

Head-count is all. It concentrates minds and amounts
to all that is real in the world.

As a ruralist from somewhere called the sticks,
provinces of the *polis*, I represent irrelevance.

What goes on here, fouled none the less, is
an abundance of weather and a few small thoughts.

Will it rain? Will it snow? Will it last?
Will we go? Will they come? Where has the post got to?

Can things go on? Things have that way with them.
But who will keep an eye on them?

The curlew and the hare? The constellations?
Who will go crying in the wilderness and why, why on earth?

Prayer

Bless those who are marginal, who only live.

Bless those whose motto is *il faut cultiver ton rêve*.

Bless those who know what lies behind the times.

An Oriental Tale

From 'The Clutag Press'

The machine has Josiah Wade, Halifax, Eng.,
stamped on its great cog, and 'ARAB' in its arch.

Even the black one-eyed stare of its ink-disk
serves the telling of an oriental tale

from Victorian Britain. Here I add to it, letter by
letter, setting a poem from the bottom up.

It reads from right to left. But then, it's true,
everything in this world is back to front.

The art lies in turning it front to back.
So I pray in my garage for the light to dawn.

Half a Loaf

A poem like life's a half-way house though
nothing can be halved that's not complete.

Half a loaf's better than no bread. A crumb of wisdom
finds a world, in a grain of wheat.

The tortoise steals for ever on the hare
while Zeno cuts a cake that isn't there.

God knows we shall be forced into retreat
and live our days out on thin air.

Elegy

'Time will take care of it, time's a great healer,'
he'd say, or: 'It wasn't meant to be,' to help you.

So you buried the dead pet unceremoniously and
wrote off overnight the girl who spurned you.

Time moved so fast in those days: blink and
you missed it. The day rose like a new rose everyday.

Yet you had time on your hands. *Ennui* was a word
at sixteen it amused you to add to your vocabulary.

When you took her boating on the lake they
called your number and said your time was up.

And you were happy to hear it, to see the sky above
and the pair of you, mirrored in the water.

Head over heels. But where is time now when you need it?
Why does it stay its hand? What is it waiting for?

What do you mean, it's biding its time? Does it
have a supply of its own it's keeping from us?

A Watched Clock

The clock once stood above a Scottish fire.
Ticking and chiming, it tolled for a world too
Busy to hear it. But still they kept observance round it,
As if it was the eye of god. Now it ticks away for us,
An antique, with a little pendulum, imported
From America: THE KENMORE made in
Connecticut by the Ansonia Clock Company, 1878.

On its face, the old man has inked in names
And dates of our tribe, spidery ghosts under glass.
He ticks them off like an assiduous obituarist,
With anecdotes. As who, in time, will tell of him?
The key to his heart's so worn now it will not
Turn the spring. But once again it's time to go. I look
Into his eye, and rising say: 'Goodbye, until…'

At Walden Pond

The finger-post pointed through the trees
Like a moment in a poem by Robert Frost.
The direction was as straight as any but
I might be walking yet and not have found it,
Or where, precisely, it once stood. I stopped,
And turned away to look down at the pond.
There a canoe of Indian design, unreal, lay
Like halves of a pea-pod, joined seamless
At the waterline: two fishermen as one fished
In two ponds. Everything in Walden woods
That day, in Walden pond in Walden sky
Swam in that plumbed blue ether-world,
Collapsing space and direction into light.
I stepped back down to walk the water's edge
And stooping (or was I reaching up?) picked
From the shore a stone, shot through with
Stars of quartz, to carry home, as if to weight
My heart's plumb-line, and bring my feet
Back to the ground, like this. To a house
I built myself, a mile from any neighbour.

The Shipwreck at Cape Cod

This scene would haunt anyone
capable of feeling: the many
marble feet and matted heads

of 'immigrants' from Galway in 1849:
famine time left unremarked
in Princeton's 'Historical Introduction'.

The drowned look out through
wide-open staring eyes, like dead-lights
or cabin windows filled with sand.

Here and there a bonnet or
a jacket, a woman's scarf, a gown,
decorates the wreck of weed.

Yet undistracted seaweed gatherers
carry off their harvest, drown who might:
why care at all for bodies?

While others cart corpses in
rough deal boxes to a hole
like a cellar: sober despatch

of business, no less moving
to his mind, the sea still
breaking violently on the rocks.

And a little further on her frail
flag spread on a rock to dry,
held down by stones at the corners.

Near Mystic

The white man comes, pale as the dawn,
With a load of thought, not guessing but
Calculating. Nations are not whimsical.
The Indian does well to continue Indian.
So driving out from Mystic, aptly, I
Pondered some pages I'd been reading.

It was a foggy morning and the woods
Kept eerie track with the road.
Their presence felt, they melted into air,
As once the Pequot must have stalked
The Yengeese. So ghostly was the way,
I nearly missed the sign to the Casino.

Spring in Charlottesville

Across a plashy green red-earthen lawn
In Charlottesville, Virginia, robins
Forayed forward, thrush-like, into March.
Half halted by the cold wet wind,
Heads cocked, they paused as, pensive,
You might pause to test a theory.

But now wild heralds sing impromptu
From bare branches to the evening,
As if to say what they proclaim is proof,
Though blossom's nipped in the bud
Better believe, who hesitates is also lost.
Adjust your clocks: this is the vernal equinox.

Birds of America

I woke again… inside a dream, startled,
On an internal flight… The navigator beside me
No sooner put his flight plan down than he
Began to show me pages out of Audubon:
The Birds of America, from Original Drawings
With 435 Plates Showing 1,065 Figures.

My first thought was that we would crash.
So many foreign objects flying. I put myself into
The brace position. But he laughed and turned
The pages: so many pages, so many birds. I could hear the air
Beat with their unnameable wings, as we descended
Into the frontier morning, where a Cardinal presided

Singing in the bushes to its heart's content.
I seemed to know at once it was a Cardinal,
A scarlet, crested, black-faced finch,
With the most melodious of voices.
I could see the sense in that, something explicable I might welcome
In the new world when I woke and clambered from the wreckage.

But suppose it had been a Grackle or
A Brown Thrasher from the Catbird family,
Would it have left me looking awry?
Or a Bobolink or a Cowbird? Scratching my head
At those queer birds, stumbling in the dark wood,
On the road less travelled, as poets should?

Blues in America

Imagine they've given you so many days,
a one-way ticket, leaving on Friday night,
or Sunday if you like, some sad régime
to see you to the gate. Even suppose you had
a choice, as to an interim destination,
where else would you set out for but
the bottom of a page like this? Or scrap you had
to hand, scoffing a burger and a latte,
at Cincinnati hub? To scrawl a poem?
But all poems must reach an end…
All bodies, friend, must come at last to earth.
I wish that mine could stay away,
believe me. I long for another fate.
I long for a form of flight on quite a different plane.
Everyday I pray things might be different.
Hitherto my references have all been local.
My compatriots regard me as *de trop* but
what has that to do with you? What has anything
to do with America but America?
I'm tired, too, of my constant recourse
to my limitations, my pared down stock
of tropes and visions. So write a line
under them and head off somewhere else?
Not elsewhere in that kneejerk sense, you jerk.
A place neither to my liking nor not,
where I have no history, and no record,
where the folk make no pretence, and every,
of having found the nearest way to truth.
A place where I've no purpose, where
I bring nothing with me to do. No
notebook in my pocket, and nothing
up my sleeve, certainly not a hanky.
A place forever where everything is new,
raw, strange, in languages I do not know.
That, itself, would be an open working
for a lifetime's poems? Given what?
The immigrants' cry that America steals their
history on entry? Or their desperate need that it should?

The usual business where you can't guess what
the givens are until they're taken from you.
Even the dispossessed have more to lose than
in the worst of worlds they ever knew? Up here,
across the continental drift of cloud-mapped plain
and dry gulch, a movie's concocting to acclaim
a gaudy patriotism, the all–American male,
the good god–fearing family… Consuming
diet Coke and pretzels, having a nice day,
we head off into ethereal frontier-light:
there seems no reason to come down.
But sure we shall descend, trailing clouds
of some or other makeshift story, some
new identity, like a badly forged passport.
I gaze upon the world below. I doze. I dream.
Already restless in my wreck of sleep, I fall
awake, and now I'm ON THE ROAD again,
cap in hand for poems, declaring:
'Here's my green card. I'd be grateful
for any tips you can give me as to…'

Appendix: Translation by Angharad Price

Y Wennol

er cof am R. S. Thomas

Muda'r nôl yn dy enw at fy nhafod i,
Ers dy fynd a'r nen yn gaeafu.

Ni allwn honni dy weld yn mynd
On noeth yn sydyn yw'r nen a'r coed cyn bo hir.

Gwag ym mhob iaith yw'r gair am ansennol
Ond am yr hyn y mae'n rhaid wrth amswer i'w ddweud.

Dim a adwaenaf, a minnau'n dy weld o hyd
Yn brigo'r cae gwair yng ngolau'r gorllewin

Ar ôl syrthio'r milltiroedd dirifedi
Dan dy gryman a thithau'n dal i droelli a gwibio

Gan ddatgan wrth y nen mai yn dragwyddol
Y gwneir gwanwyn, anghofiwch haf a gaeaf y galon.

Notes

Plato's Aviary (Puts out a Wing)
This group of poems is a continuation or an extension of the twenty-three
'Plato's Aviary' poems in *Nevermore*. They play upon Socrates's use in the
Theaetetus of the 'aviary' as a figure for the mind, memory and recall.

Arboretum
The trees and other plants included here are those that stand for the letters
in the Irish tree-alphabet, though the poems are not deployed in tree-
alphabetic order, but as they might best afford variety together. Of a
handful of possible 'modern' variants, 'Briar' is the only one I have
included, in preference to 'Vine'. The background to all this may be found
in Robert Graves's *The White Goddess* (1948, edited by Grevel Lindop,
Carcanet Press 1997, chapters 10 and 11). The epigraph to 'Silver-Fir' from
Kierkegaard is as quoted in *Six Existentialist Thinkers* (Routledge, 1961) by
H. J. Blackham (a book read by the 'playboy' in the poem 'Meditation in
Homage to the Playboy' here). The two-line 'Ivy' is taken direct from the
Latin inscription on the self-portrait in the National Gallery, London, of
Salvatore Rosa (1615–73).

Allt
'Tan yr Allt' means 'under the wooded hill'. 'Ar hyd yr nos' means 'all
through the night' and alludes to the famous hymn of that name. 'Ar lan y
môr' means 'On the seashore' and is the title of a traditional Welsh air:

Ar lan y môr mae rhosys cochion	[On the seashore there are red roses]
Ar lan y môr mae lilys gwynion	[there are white lilies]
Ar lan y môr mae 'nghariad inne	[is my sweetheart]
Yn cysgu'r nos a chodi'r bore	[Sleeping nights and rising morning]
Ar lan y môr mae cerrig gleision	[On the seashore there are blue stones [pebbles]]
Ar lan y môr mae blodau'r meibion	[are the flower of young manhood]
Ar lan y môr mae pob rhinwedde	[is every virtue]
Ar lan y môr mae 'nghariad inne	[is my sweetheart]
Mor hardd yw'r haul yn codi'r bore	[So beautiful is the sun at morning rising]
Mor hardd yw'r enfys aml ei liwie	[So beautiful is the rainbow of various colours]
Mor hardd yw natur ym Mehefin	[So beautiful is nature in June]
On harddwch fyth yw wyneb Elin	[But eternal beauty is Elin's face]

Launched in October 1957, 'Sputnik' (Russian for travelling-companion) was the first man-made satellite successfully to orbit earth. It was clearly visible to the naked eye, and a great excitement to see, as it journeyed over the Welsh coast and the mountains of Snowdonia. 'Tan-yr-Allt' marched with the Mostyn Estate at Gloddaeth where Bryn Maelgwyn stands.

Croeso
The word is Welsh for 'welcome'.

After Taliesin
For more concerning Taliesin, the sixth-century Welsh poet see the poem 'Allt'. The first line of this poem derives from the Book of Genesis, the last line is William Blake's. For 'The spit of seals' see the poem here 'Smogairle Rōin', and for the *Naomh Eanna* see *Nevermore*, and for 'Not a pair of pampooties' see *An Aran Keening* (see next note).

At Roundstone
Tim Robinson is the author of the two classic volumes *Stones of Aran* (1986, 1995), as well as other brilliant essays on the topography and cultural history of the Burren in Co. Clare and of Connemara. He and his wife Máiréad lived for several years on Inis Mór, where they settled in 1972. The poem celebrates our first meeting, in the company of our mutual friend and publisher Antony Farrell of the Lilliput Press Ltd, Dublin. The encounter, at Roundstone in Connemara, was occasioned by Lilliput's publication in March 2001 of *An Aran Keening*, an account of my sojourn on Inis Mór, November 1968-September 1969, reviewed the day of our meeting by Tim Robinson in the *Irish Times*. The phrase 'another island haunter' refers to the Scottish poet Hugh MacDiarmid. He lived for nine years on Whalsay in the Shetlands and produced much of his finest poetry there. His lines about 'meaning' and 'value' may be found in the poems 'In Memoriam: Liam Mac ´Ille Iosa' and 'Lament for the Great Music' in the volume *Stony Limits* (1934). 'Folding Landscapes' is the name of the imprint under which the Robinsons publish their maps of the Burren, Aran, and Connemara, vital productions that trace these dramatically beautiful territories back into their Irish-speaking history.

The Blacksmith's Order Centenary
John McNeillie (1865–1941), my great-grandfather, began his working life as a blacksmith and became a tenant farmer, at North Clutag, a remote steading in Wigtownshire, in the ancient kingdom of Galloway. My father John McNeillie (1916–2002), spent the greater part of his infancy and

childhood at North Clutag, raised by his grandparents and aunts. For the matter regarding the immortality of the plough, compare 'You told me the plough was immortal!' from 'Stony Grey Soil' by Patrick Kavanagh. The reference to Darwin is to Robin Darwin, great-grandson of Charles, who created the cover illustration for my father's first novel *Wigtown Ploughman: Part of His Life* (Putnam, 1939). Bladnoch Distillery on the Bladnoch River at Wigtown still produces Scotland's most southerly (and best of all) malt whisky. *The Works of Virgil. Translated by John Dryden*, referred to here, was a volume in the Chandos Classics Series: 'Reprinted from the best editions with Memoir &c' by Frederick Warne and Co., London and New York, n.d. For the 'iron age' or age of iron see Virgil's fourth Eclogue.

The Shipwreck at Cape Cod
This poem makes very direct use of Henry David Thoreau's essay 'The Shipwreck' (1855), later included in the posthumous collection *Cape Cod* (1865).

Near Mystic
The first four lines of this poem come directly from Thoreau's *A Week on the Concord and Merrimac Rivers* (1849), the essay on 'Sunday': 'The white man comes, pale as the dawn, with a load of thought, with a slumbering intelligence as a fire raked up, knowing well what he knows, not guessing but calculating; strong in community, yielding obedience to authority; of experienced race; of wonderful, wonderful common sense; dull but capable, slow but persevering, severe but just, of little humour but genuine; a labouring man, despising game and sport; building a house that endures, a framed house. He buys the Indian's moccasins and baskets, then buys his hunting-grounds, and at length forgets where he is buried and ploughs up his bones... He comes with a list of ancient Saxon, Norman, and Celtic names, and strews them up and down this river – Framingham, Sudbury, Bedford, Carlisle, Billericay, Chelmsford – and this is New Angle-land, and these are the New West Saxons whom the Red Men call, not Angle-ish or English, but Yengeese, and so at last they are known for Yankees... If we could listen but for an instant to the chant of the Indian muse, we should understand why he will not exchange his savageness for civilization. Nations are not whimsical. Steel and blankets are strong temptations; but the Indian does well to continue Indian.'